# WONDERFUL WALLCOVERINGS

Laura May Todd

Lannoo

# INTRODUCTION

——

## THE NEW WORLD OF WALLCOVERING

Wallcovering is not what it used to be. Forget your preconceptions about dated rolls of dusty wallpaper, because they are a thing of the past. Today's wallcoverings are artful textiles made of inventive materials and wrought by skilled craftsmanship. In recent years there has been an explosion of interest in this new generation of wallcoverings. They have become more sophisticated and design trends lean towards the maximal once again. The past few years have seen a resurgence of colour, pattern and print in the interiors world. Flip open the pages of any of the major design magazines and you will be greeted with bold walls, brightly upholstered furniture and vibrant mixes of texture and print. As you can imagine, there is no better decorative element to express these new trends on a grand scale than wallcovering.

But that wasn't always the case. As design trends evolve from one decade to the next, certain styles fall in and out of fashion. Several years past, minimal tastes dominated the trend cycles, and all-white walls with neutral furnishings were the luxury styling du jour. But as happens with every trend, the pendulum eventually swings the other way – and it certainly has.

## WALLCOVERINGS IN THE PAST

The resurgence of wallcovering comes as no surprise. As far back as the Middle Ages, the upper classes were using finely wrought tapestries as insulation in their draughty castles and cavernous palaces. In fact, early wallpapers were merely imitations of these prohibitively expensive wall hangings. Such intricately woven textiles were available only to the very wealthy, so enterprising artisans began to mimic them with ink and paper using block-printing techniques, in which an image would be carved onto a piece of wood, the block would be inked, and the image would be transferred onto a sheet of paper.

Over the following centuries, wallpaper became ubiquitous. By the nineteenth century, all but the most humble homes were lined with decadently decorative wallpaper. By the mid-1800s, technology had advanced to the point where the mass production of wallpaper became possible, which opened the floodgates for new experimentation in patterns and styles. Everything from trompe-l'œil effects that mimic natural materials, to chinoiserie-inspired scenes, chintz floral patterns and prints inspired by textiles was lining the walls during that era. This was the time of William Morris and his Arts and Crafts movement compatriots, who created lusciously illustrated patterns that depicted the natural world and remain popular even today. The arrival of newly available products on the market also encouraged new methods of hanging wallpaper to maximise the amount of pattern one enjoys in each room. Victorian decorators were mixing as many as three different types of wallpaper per room – above and beneath the chair rail and along the edge of the ceiling – for an overwhelmingly print-heavy effect that stayed in fashion for many years.

Moving into the twentieth century, patterns became noticeably more restrained. Homeowners in the conservative 1950s preferred 'flat, linear patterns and abstract geometric motifs, only to see them replaced by an explosion of bright colour and hallucinogenic Op and Pop designs in the 1960s' ('A Brief History of Wallpaper', V&A). It wasn't until the 1980s that the popularity of wallpaper began to wane as consumers shifted their interest to different wall-decoration techniques, such as Venetian plaster and cloudy sponge-finished painted walls.

As all trends are, the popularity of wallcovering has been cyclical. But the interest from designers and their clients is growing once again, with a few notable differences in taste. There is a new desire for more artisan and handmade products, and a fresh curiosity has been sparked into the potential of unconventional materials and techniques. That has pushed contemporary artisans into discovering totally new ways to create wallcoverings.

## MATERIAL MATTERS

In many ways, wallcoverings that are available now more closely resemble the laboriously crafted wall hangings of centuries past. In the same way that garment manufacturers are continuously on the lookout for new, sustainable textiles to replace the older, less environmentally friendly ones, the producers of wallcoverings have discovered a plethora of new materials to use. It is now possible to find wallcoverings in genuine cowhide leather, seashells, the bark of the banana tree, water hyacinth leaves, sisal, soft suede, raw jute, rope, rattan – the list goes on.

Many of the new materials on the market not only are prized for their sustainable qualities, but also open up an entire world of texture and colour to enable interior designers and architects to enhance their projects. Take, for instance, banana leaves. Bananas are the fourth-largest food crop in the world and grow incredibly quickly. But in the past, once the fruit was harvested, the mother trunk and leaves were left to decompose. To reduce waste, the leaves have begun to be harvested be turned into usable materials. Artisans will cut the wide banana let into narrow strips and leave them to harden and dry. The resulting materials can be coloured and woven with sturdy threads to create a unique wallcovering.

Another natural material that artisans have begun to experiment with is Capiz, an oyster-like shell. These shells are grown underwater and they are undeniably beautiful — each one has a unique colour, structure and shape. Capiz can be found in the Indian Ocean and the Pacific, and — for this wallcovering — the shells are harvested near Samal, an island in the Philippines. Once collected, the shells are individually painted, cut and inlaid in geometric patterns. What makes this material even more special to work with is that the colour nuances of the mother-of-pearl vary according to the light, creating a constantly changing effect that varies from room to room and every hour of the day. All these different elements make Capiz a perfect medium to create some of the most artistic and exclusive wallcovering there is.

Banana leaf and Capiz are just two of the many experimental materials that artisans are working with in the world of contemporary wallcoverings.

## WONDERFUL WALLCOVERINGS

Contemporary styles are worlds away from the patterns that were popular in decades past. The latest wallcoverings to enter the market come in so many interesting styles and designs: there are 3D patterns for when you need to add some texture to a space, panoramic illustrations that resemble hand-painted murals, finely wrought tapestry-like textiles and earthy natural materials, to name a few.

In the pages of this book, we have compiled a wealth of interiors with creative wallcoverings from some of the most interesting designers working, organised into six chapters that best illustrate the trends most popular today. 'Flora & Fauna', is a contemporary take on the patterns depicting the natural world first popularised in the 1800s. Then things calm down a little with 'Staying Neutral', which provides a helpful primer on how to use wallcovering even within an otherwise toned-down aesthetic. 'The Art of the Pattern Clash,' is a bold selection that takes us through daring interiors that aren't afraid to mix and match their eye-popping prints. From there we move on to 'Maximal Thinking', a parade of extroverted spaces that make the most of bold patterns and 'Modern Elegance', a series of refined rooms in rich colours. Finally, we end things with 'Graphic Touches', a contemporary look at the ever-classic accent wall. We hope that by exploring these pages, you find inspiration, education and a new appreciation for the wonderful world of wallcoverings.

# TABLE OF CONTENTS

——

CHAPTER 1

## FLORA & FAUNA

16 — Mexican grandeur in California

22 — Children's bedrooms with extra spark

28 — Adventure through antiques and souvenirs

34 — Elaborate patterns in a subtle palette

40 — Framed cranes as pieces of art

46 — Playful flat full of contrast

50 — Sumptuous bar and lounge

56 — Interview Traci Connell

CHAPTER 2

## STAYING NEUTRAL

60 — Pinks and pales for the ice-cream shop

66 — Historical space with design of today

72 — At home in the office

78 — Forest hideaway

86 — Luxurious, eco-friendly villa

92 — Subtle shades of grey

98 — Interview Kris Turnbull

CHAPTER 3

## THE ART OF THE PATTERN CLASH

102 — Decadent layered patterns

108 — Room of contrasts

114 — Differentiate spaces by wallpaper

120 — Multiple motifs mixed

126 — Bold, playful, and risqué

132 — Interview Daniel Meloché and Joanna Kado

CHAPTER 4

# MAXIMAL THINKING

136 — Wondrous living room

140 — Modern art deco bar

146 — Industrial meets speakeasy

152 — Basement bar

158 — Natural class

164 — A world journey within a restaurant

168 — Interview Christie Wright

CHAPTER 5

# MODERN ELEGANCE

172 — Glamorous autumn

178 — Luxe and low-key hotel

184 — Functional luxury

190 — Historic hotel with contemporary features

194 — Playful home office

198 — Creative workspace

204 — The notary's house

208 — Interview Linda Lagrand

CHAPTER 6

# GRAPHIC TOUCHES

212 — Luxury farmhouse

216 — Art on display

222 — The ceiling sets the tone

228 — Colour-blocked hotel room

232 — Eclectic accent wall

236 — A speakeasy bar

240 — Golden eye-catcher

244 — Edgy denim wallcovering

248 — Natural touches

252 — Interview Adriana Nicolau

# FLORA

—

CHAPTER 1

—

# & FAUNA

Vibrant patterns that invite the natural world in

# MEXICAN GRANDEUR IN CALIFORNIA

—

The designers of the Mexican restaurant Esperanza in California's Manhattan Beach wanted to channel 'the grandeur of a villa in Mexico' for the design concept, which also evokes a moody, speakeasy vibe. To achieve this look, they opted for dark colours and an all-over wallpaper look that totally envelops the guests. 'The decor and design pieces blur lines between art and function. The second floor of the restaurant contains a secret bar inspired by a sensuous home where the best secret party in town will take place,' explain the designers.

For the project, they chose a lush jungle motif bursting with tropical birds, exotic flowers and lurking animals. 'This particular wallcovering is very unique,' they add. 'It creates an intimate mood and makes you feel like you are in a jungle-themed hideaway.' Rather than keeping that vivacious pattern confined to just the walls, they papered the ceiling and bar as well. The effect is unquestionably dramatic and makes visitors feel as if they have set foot in a secret tropical escape.

—

**DESIGNER**
Gulla Jónsdóttir from
Atelier Gulla Jónsdóttir

—

**LOCATION**
United States

By covering the walls, ceiling and bar with the same
bold print, the space becomes immediately intimate, as
if one is stepping into a secret underground speakeasy.
When working with such a vivacious and busy pattern,
it often pays to go big.

# CHILDREN'S BEDROOMS WITH EXTRA SPARK

——

Creating a space for a child is a very special task. It needs to be comfortable and soothing, while ideally having an extra spark of playfulness to ignite their creativity. This is exactly what designer Maartje Diepstraten did when she came up with the concept for these children's bedrooms in Belgium. For each child's room, she chose a gorgeous wallpaper print full of life and wonder. The first features curling vines and blooming flowers, while the second is an all-blue motif featuring playfully stomping elephants. These understated patterns are good examples of updated versions of classic children's decor, in that they do not feel overly gendered, while the vintage-feeling design is perfect for longevity as there will be no need to redecorate as the children grow.

'I chose this wallpaper because of the colours, the print and the beautiful quality,' explains Diepstraten. 'The print seems quite strong, but because of the colours it isn't overkill, and it actually works really well.' The choice of print fits well into Diepstraten's broader concept for the design, in which she blends different elements in an almost casual way. 'When it comes to decorating a room or an entire house, I just use a few key elements that I like and then collect smaller items round those that make it a whole. I think that if you have a clear idea for yourself of what you think is beautiful, all the elements that you collect throughout the years, from a couch to the wallpaper, will meld together nicely.'

——
**DESIGNER**
Maartje Diepstraten
from Barts Boekje

——
**LOCATION**
The Netherlands

To strike a balance between playful and peaceful, the designer chose to cover the wall closest to the window with this delightful elephant-patterned wallcovering, a placement that ensures it receives ample natural light. By painting the adjacent wall a pale shade of grey, the otherwise busy room – filled with toys, clothes and various textiles – is imbued with a sense of order and calm.

# ADVENTURE THROUGH ANTIQUES AND SOUVENIRS

—

'The interior of every home should tell its owner's story and express their passion,' states designer Günel Aghazada about her recent makeover of a house in Dubai. 'This is a renovation of a house recently purchased by a young family who are starting their dream home journey. To start the story, our initial concept was based on the clients' love of nature, cultural heritage and travel history. As they have an existing collection of art, special souvenirs and curiosities, as well as furniture including antique pieces, the task was to incorporate that into the new interior, which leads visitors on a discovery adventure within the space.'

Aghazada brought out the owners' personalities with a series of tropical-themed wallpapers. In the entranceway, visitors are greeted with leafy-green palm fronds and colourful yellow parrots. In the kitchen, amber-coloured monkeys scramble across a forest scene, which matches cleverly placed monkey pendant lamps. In the bathroom, peacocks fan their elaborate feathers in Japanese gardens in shades of dark inky blue. 'The wallpaper tells a story,' adds Aghazada, describing the whirlwind world tour depicted on the walls. 'It is a great tool to tell a story and guide the adventure we were trying to create.'

—
**DESIGNER**
Günel Aghazada

—
**LOCATION**
United Arab Emirates

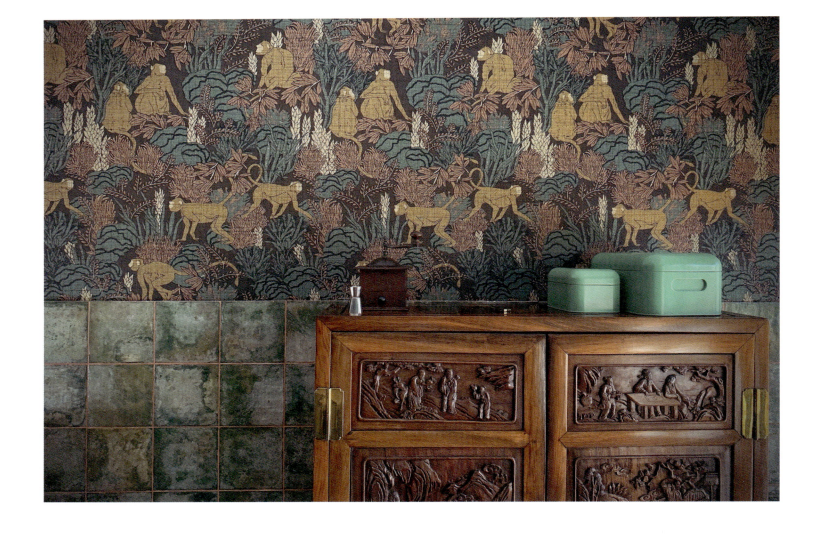

It may seem counterintuitive to line a small room that receives little natural light with a dark patterned wallcovering, but the results are likely to surprise you. Rather than feeling busy or overpowering, the effect is instead welcoming – perfect for an intimate space such as a guest bathroom.

# ELABORATE PATTERNS IN A SUBTLE PALETTE

—

This stylish apartment in Paris shows that a pattern-forward design need not be overpowering. In fact, the wallpaper used by interior architect Candice Bruny illustrates that even when mixing elaborate patterns, a room can be calm, welcoming and serene. Candice undertook this renovation for a young couple who wanted to better utilise the period apartment's spatial dimensions and gorgeous original features, such as parquet flooring. 'The owner wished to transform and modernise the apartment, so as to obtain more clear and functional volumes,' explains Candice, who created a large open kitchen, two bedrooms, a large bathroom and an office.

Candice picked a gentle tropical theme for the private spaces – specifically, the bedroom and office – in order to bring some texture and colour to the otherwise subtle palette. In the bedroom, she used a pale-blue flamingo motif to lead the eye towards the bed, the visual centrepiece of the room. Meanwhile, she washed the office in a shade of forest green by applying a playful palm-frond pattern on just the top half of the wall so as not to overwhelm the small space with print. 'It reinforces the personal aspect of an interior,' she explains of the choice, 'and brings together the interesting materials, texture and originality of the decoration.'

**DESIGNER**
Candice Bruny

**LOCATION**
France

Candice's design of the office emulates more traditional wall decoration, in which a chair rail, wainscoting and wallpaper would be installed together, though in this case with an entirely contemporary spin. The same proportions remain, but Candice opted for a sleek brass rail and did away with conventional crown moulding for a pared-back and modern look.

# FRAMED CRANES AS PIECES OF ART

——

A vibrantly patterned wallpaper is an excellent tool for creating a sophisticated colour story, even within a space that is predominantly neutral. Case in point, Balo Bar in Hasselt, Belgium, where the designers enhanced an otherwise monochromatic interior with a bright pop of cherry red in the form of a patterned series of panels. Throughout the stylish bar, shades of grey dominate — across the bar, walls and sleek banquette — but the choice of red totally elevates the design.

'The pattern is made up of cranes in flight, which are deemed genuine lucky charms in a number of countries,' the designers explain of their choice of pattern, which they hung in frames round the bar area like pieces of art. They then placed a pair of upholstered seats in a similar shade of red directly in front, creating a dialogue in colour between the opposite sides of the bar. 'Not only is this design a treat for the eye,' they go on to say, 'but the materials are also very tactile. The patterns are embroidered onto a cotton and linen fabric, a blend yielding an opulent finish.'

——
**DESIGNER**
Balo Design Boutique

——
**LOCATION**
Belgium

Confining a wallcovering to picture frames allows for an element of flexibility within a space. If the furniture needs to be rearranged, the framed wallcoverings can be moved to better reflect the new interior configuration.

# PLAYFUL FLAT FULL OF CONTRAST

—

'In this apartment lives a fashionista with fantastic taste,' says interior designer Linda Lagrand. 'We helped her pick the wallpaper and curtains, and some small furniture and accessories to complete her own collection.' The overall vibe of this playful apartment is one of contrasts, both youthful and fun, but with a sophisticated twist: the ideal bachelorette pad. In choosing the wallcovering, Lagrand took two very different routes for the dressing room, where the owner keeps her impressive collection of clothing and accessories, and for the living room, which is set up to entertain.

'In the dressing room, the wallpaper functions as a lush green backdrop for the collection of fashion items of the resident,' says Lagrand, who covered the walls with a fresh fern pattern that makes the room feel bright and calm. She continued with the palette of natural materials by adding a rattan pendant light and a potted bamboo plant in the corner. In the living room, however, she kept things neutral. There, the walls are covered with a grey woven textile covering, which makes a wonderful backdrop for the sophisticated mid-century furniture. Altogether, it is the perfect apartment for a fashion-forward young woman.

—
**DESIGNER**
Linda Lagrand

—
**LOCATION**
The Netherlands

When choosing the decoration for their walls, most homeowners aren't interested in all-over print, which can often feel overwhelming. Adding neutral areas, like here in the living room, provides balance. However, neutral doesn't necessarily mean flat – this textile wallcovering adds a sense of richness and texture to the room.

# SUMPTUOUS BAR AND LOUNGE

—

The Kips Bay Decorator Show House is an annual event organised as both an interior design showcase and a charity project. Each year, designers across the country collaboratively decorate a mansion in a way that encapsulates the mood of the moment and often dictates the trends going forward the following year. A recent edition saw American designer Traci Connell create a sumptuous bar and lounge within the house which centred on the richly patterned walls.

Starting with the seating area, which featured a forest scene in shades of pale purple, blues and greys, 'a focal point in the space is the flocked wall mural that resembles a moody, lush tropic,' explains Connell. 'As a rainforest is characterised by many ecosystems living under one continuous tree canopy, so too is the space multifaceted with a double bar area to refresh your martini and a free-form banquette to rest your feet, inspired by the natural bamboo of the rainforest - which sits in front of the flocked wall mural that evokes the ambience of a rich and tangled jungle.'

—
**DESIGNER**
Traci Connell Interiors

—
**LOCATION**
United States

The soft illustration on the walls cleverly contrasts with the straight lines of the wooden fluted panels, adding a sense of depth to the boldly decorated room.

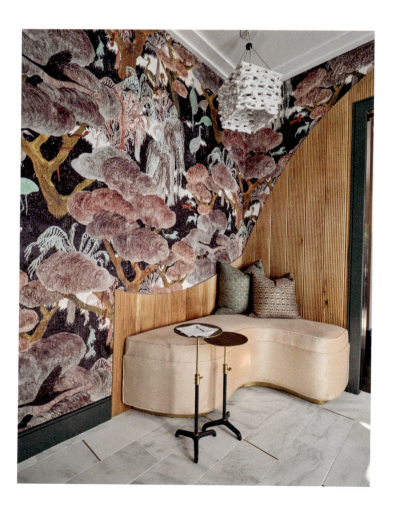

# TRACI CONNELL

Traci Connell is an award-winning, nationally published interior designer. Her luxury, namesake design firm is based in Dallas, Texas, and serves clients across the United States. Over the years, the Traci Connell Interiors team has perfected and streamlined a system of service that simplifies and organises the design process, becoming one of the most trusted design firms in Dallas.

—

**SUMPTUOUS
BAR AND LOUNGE**
United States

—

**When working with such a bold-patterned wallcovering, how do you design a room – for example, choosing the colour palette and other finishings – round the print?**
We always start with pinpointing colours in the paper that we want to accent, then pulling rugs, paint swatches and other fabrics to start to form a theme or colour palette. Once we have landed on our perfect marriage, we are always in tune with the scale of patterns. If the wallpaper has a very large-scale pattern, we tend to tone down the other patterns. It's very important to not take away from the beauty of the main piece!

**What are your top tips for creating a space for entertaining within a home?**
Entertaining spaces may just be our favourite! Hence the pool bar and bath we designed for Kips Bay. We make sure that everything we design is functional, and offers the owner ease of use. Popping accent walls with wallpaper is our favourite, so we may choose a vinyl paper for the bar wall, or possibly steer away from grasscloth if the wall has a lot of curves, et cetera. But when entertaining, we like to always give each space a purpose - whether it is lounging, chatting, eating or multifunctional. The way we accomplish that is by utilising finishes – that is, wallpaper – to delineate the rooms.

**What are your tips for mixing strong textures and strong prints?**
Textures are a wonderful way to add pattern without actually having to add a pattern. In our designs we never shy away from a bold pattern or texture. Most important is that you pay attention to the scale and the placement of the prints. Choose well thought out locations for the strong prints that are paired with a strong texture on a different medium. For example, if the strong print is on the wallcovering, choose furniture pieces to accent the strong texture. A wallpaper with a strong texture can read as a solid with incredible depth which is why textured wallpapers are always our go-to. We can pair it with a strong print in a fun pillow elsewhere in the room!

# STAYING

—

CHAPTER 2

—

# NEUTRAL

Understated spaces with a big impact

# PINKS AND PALES FOR THE ICE-CREAM SHOP

—

The delicate mix of pale pinks and creams becomes the perfect background for this ice-cream shop in Uelsen, Germany. With such a soft and understated palette to work with, the designer, Charlotte te Wierik from Interior Vitamins (on freelance base for Valk Design), focused on texture to create visual interest within the space, contrasting a moulded ceiling with wooden fluted walls, a smartly tiled bar and a subtle, diamond-printed wallpaper. 'This ice-cream boutique had to become a space full of exciting contrasts,' says the designer. 'Both in style, classic and modern, but also in the combination of colours and materials. In this way, a strong image is created, but there is still a great balance.'

The effect of the wallpaper is really what gives this ice-cream shop a playful but sophisticated punch, creating an almost trompe-l'œil effect similar to textured plaster or boiserie. While the pale shade of pink works to imbue the space with a sense of cosiness, 'the warm colour tones, with their graphic pattern, give a modern touch to the boutique,' she adds.

—

**DESIGNER**
Interior Vitamins

—

**LOCATION**
Germany

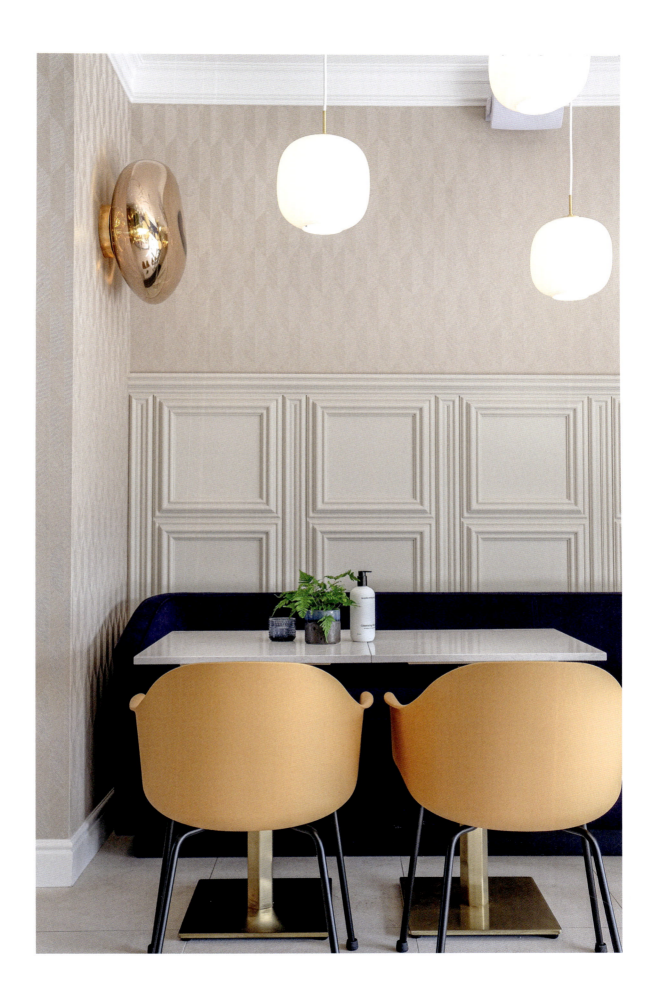

A straightforward painted wall would have fallen flat in such a richly layered yet subtle space. The faint diamond pattern of the woven wallcovering creates the perfect amount of contrast when set against the stronger profile of the moulded walls and ceiling.

# HISTORICAL SPACE WITH DESIGN OF TODAY

—

The concept for this VIP airport lounge in Salzburg was multifaceted. The designers were tasked with channelling the historical design of the previous iteration of the lounge. Or, as they put it, 'draw a line between the history of thirty years of the airport and the design of today'. They were also asked to pay homage to regional traditions native to Salzburg, including materials and design elements. 'The idea of the designer was to create an elegant and classy but still warm and cosy feeling in this VIP area,' explain the designers. 'The colours used are soft and smooth, with a little touch of purple in the chairs and the couch to mix it up.'

They chose a sophisticated wallpaper with a hexagonal motif in pale beige and white that resembles inlaid stone. 'In a tasteful way, the wallpaper looks like sand-coloured natural stone which was taken from the local area of Salzburg,' they explain regarding their design choice. 'For the customer, it was important to use regional materials. The wallpaper adds the distinguishing international touch to the overall design, combining regionality with modernity, characteristics which an airport also represents.'

—
**DESIGNER**
Derenko Interior
Design

—
**LOCATION**
Austria

The dark stained wood and subtle
wallcovering motif in this airport
lounge make a typically anonymous
public space feel warm and welcoming.

# AT HOME IN THE OFFICE

—

The owners of this newly renovated office space, set in a historic former home in Amsterdam's Vondelpark, wanted to maintain the homey feel. The brief they gave designer Maaike van Diemen was to create 'an office to live in,' she says. 'This gave me the opportunity to use more bold materials. I wanted to do right to the character of the building, and also make a beautiful combination of the classical appearance of the building and the more modern, surprising elements.'

Van Diemen went about this by dressing the walls in shades of grey. In the living room, a horizontal pattern with a slight gradient woven into the textile is the perfect match for tall ceilings with crown moulding and pale parquet wooden floors. While in the conference room, she used the same motif, but in a darker shade. This pattern harmonises beautifully with the playful dotted motif in the adjoining space, which acts as a sitting room complete with comfortable sectional sofa. 'This wallpaper gives a luxurious and calm appearance,' van Diemen says of her choices. 'Because the pattern is woven directly into the wallcovering it makes the room a bit more exciting. The colours add beautifully to the other colours in the room and the carpet.'

—
**DESIGNER**
Maaike van Diemen

—
**LOCATION**
The Netherlands

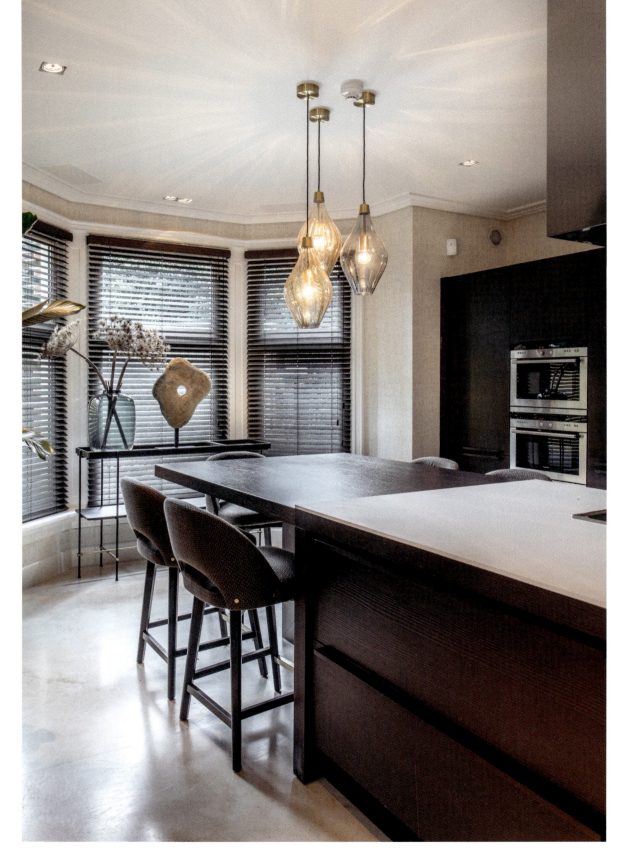

The spaces throughout the house were kept open plan and fluid, but wallpaper played a key role in differentiating between them. 'The wallpaper makes for a beautiful combination with the other materials in the interior – for example, with the carpets and classic woodwork,' she adds. 'Using wallcoverings with a different pattern in several rooms gives each space a more unique character.

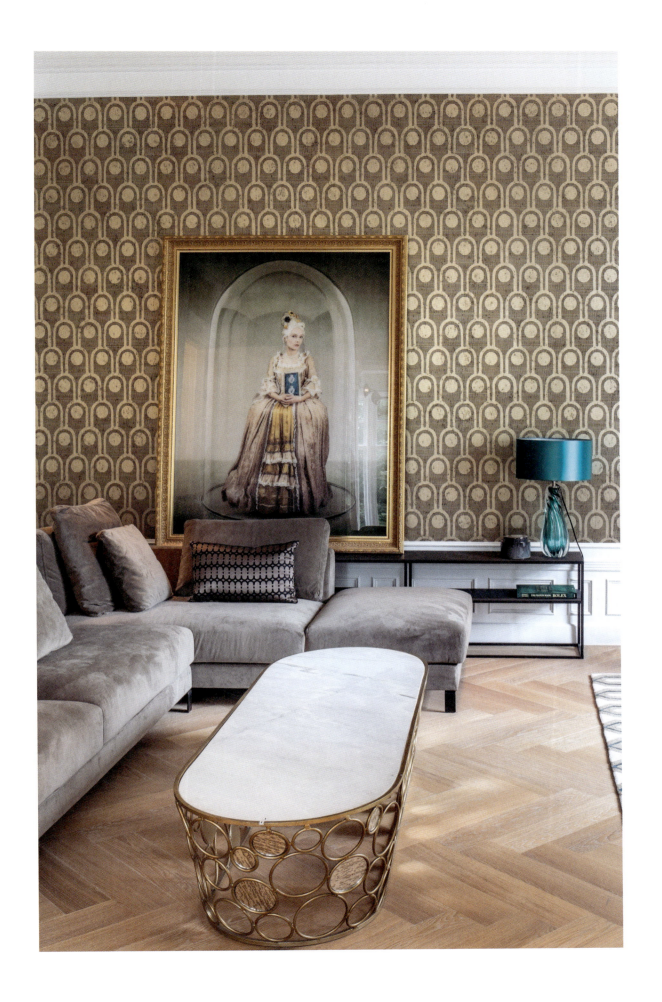

# FOREST HIDEAWAY

—

This elegant getaway in Belgium was imagined as an escape for the owners. Set over two floors and overlooking a dense forest, the spaces are designed for both relaxation and entertaining. In the living room, for instance, the owners have created a multipurpose entertainment space defined by a curving sectional sofa, a playful mix of textiles and wooden ceiling beams reminiscent of an old country barn. 'In the living room, we used a more vibrant wallcovering pattern, which gives the room a shiny and outspoken touch,' reveal the designers, who chose a pale-pink wallcovering with metallic flecks, which complements the lustre of the gold-toned accessories and luscious rose-coloured velvet sofa.

'The combination of the colours of the wallcovering, along with the rest of the space, allows the rooms to flow seamlessly into one another,' they continue. In order to create this sense of consistency, the designers used a 3D wallcovering that resembles fluted plaster as a neutral accent wall in the various rooms, as well as in the in-between spaces of the house, such as the hallways and stairwell, which allowed the spaces to flow easily. As for the smaller family room, which they call the 'chill-out room', they opted for a pink-and-brown graphic pattern that feels intimate and warm. 'For the wallpaper in the chill room of the house,' they add, 'the purpose was to give the space a cosy, warm and secure feel.'

—
**DESIGNER**
Studio de Blieck

—
**LOCATION**
Belgium

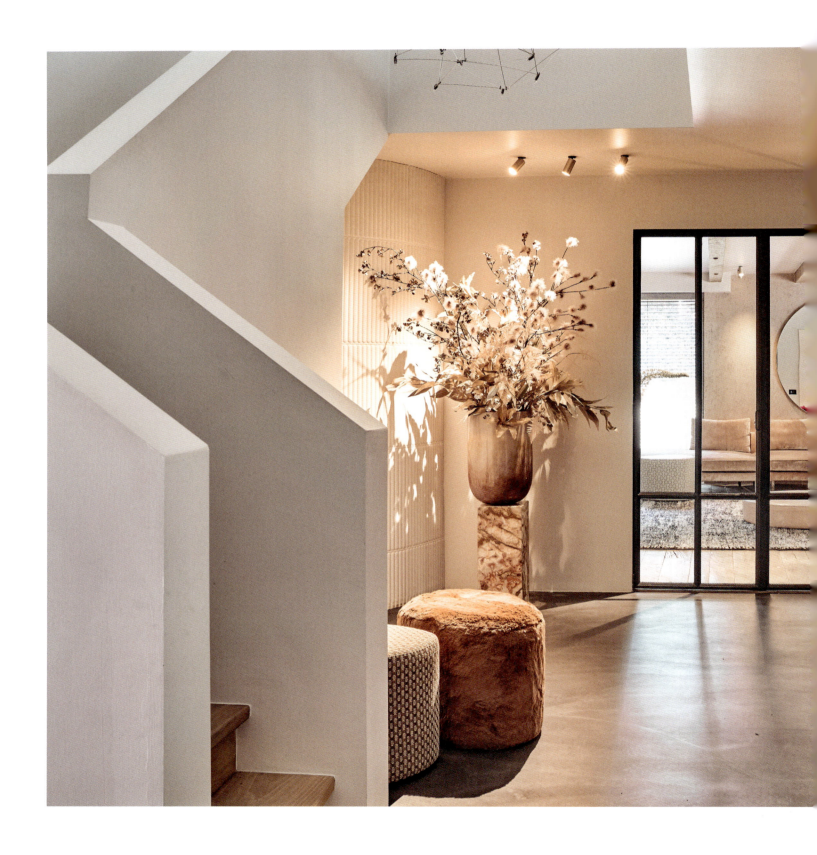

The textured 3D wallcovering that lines the hallway and foyer adds a sense of warmth within the space while also having a positive effect on the acoustics of the home. The wallcovering makes sounds softer and less reverberant.

# LUXURIOUS, ECO-FRIENDLY VILLA

—

Simbithi Eco-Estate is a sustainable residence in South Africa conceptual-ised by M&M Designs. Overlooking the luscious greenery of the surrounding area, the overall design of the space is simultaneously delicate and rich, with a decadent mix of materials and textures. 'This home's architecture inspired an interior that is modern and grand,' said the designers, who decorated the walls in a subtle pointillist graphic pattern that resembles a cloudy motif when viewed from afar. The wallpaper's light-grey shades were then extended throughout the space — from the textiles to the cabinet fronts, upholstered furniture and grey-veined marble sink — creating a soft but nuanced palette that allows the stunning views outside the window to take centre stage.

'Our clients' brief called for a luxurious modern home set with timeless elements, something we achieved through the generous use of space, exquisite modern art and touches of brass throughout,' they add. Indeed, in the kitchen they incorporated the metallic palette in the form of a bright, brass-toned accent wall in a burnished-metal motif, which visually separates the kitchen from the adjacent dining areas.

—

**DESIGNER**
M&M Designs

—

**LOCATION**
South Africa

In the primary bathroom, the designers chose to pair a wallcovering with soft patterns in almost the same grey tone as the paint of the walls to create a subtle sense of contrast.

# SUBTLE SHADES OF GREY

——

It's not always the case that walls need bright colours to make a big impact. Sometimes, subtlety can be just as strong. Such is the case in this luxurious London villa by designer Kris Turnbull, who used tactility and tone to create a calming and sophisticated retreat. Throughout the home, Turnbull used shades of grey in various textures. Grey features in the sleek wood flooring in the kitchen, the soft sectional sofa and plush carpet in the living room, and, of course, the wallcovering, which expertly ties together the different rooms.

'As the space is overexposed with natural light and a quantity of glass, the wallcovering was selected to showcase itself as a unique objet, a pure and texturised silk weave,' Kris Turnbull explains of his choice, a woven textile wallcovering with a slight gradient. For the furnishing, he sourced pieces that would blend easily with the walls, choosing a white marble table with veining in a similar shade of grey and abstract art that also works within the chosen palette. He then lined the ceiling with a reflective metallic covering that resembles silver leaf, which plays against the walls' softer finish to add a sense of dynamism within the room.

——

**DESIGNER**
Kris Turnbull Studios

——

**LOCATION**
United Kingdom

In the bathroom, Kris Turnbull followed the same medium-grey palette, using a wallcovering with a braided motif to provide a subtle juxtaposition to the similarly toned chevron-patterned marble tiles in the shower.

All together, moving through the rooms of the elegantly appointed home, the consistency of the palette in tandem with the different textures works to create a subdued sense of luxury.

# KRIS
# TURNBULL

——

Founded in 2007, Kris Turnbull Studios is a high-end architectural and luxury interior design studio specialising in residential projects for private clients and property developers round the world. Dedicated to designing through the eyes of each client, Kris and his creative team approach every commission in a tailored fashion backed by extensive property and design experience, award-winning developments and a natural eye for luxury.

—
**SUBTLE SHADES
OF GREY**
United Kingdom
—

**The project, in the designer's words:**
The client brief was to design and build a contemporary extension to the rear of the property, connecting the new landscape garden to achieve a sense of flow from inside to outside & reimagine the family lifestyle space to include a new kitchen, dining and lounge to entertain family and friends.

**In general, how can wallcovering enhance the design of a space?**
Wallcovering has come a very long way. In Ireland, wallcovering was deemed a traditional and classical approach to interiors, yet the scope of materials and stunning technical details used now can create a phenomenal transformation for an interior. When creating interior space, layering is what gives texture, depth and a sense of luxury to an interior, especially that of a more contemporary style. Wallcovering adds curiosity and interest and gives a sense of feeling. Wallcovering, often the subtlety of it, is the secret!

**Take us through the design process of choosing the wallcovering for the project.**
The design is approached in a holistic manner, designing from the inside out. Working with the in-house team of architects and interior designers, we create the perfect internal space building the architectural structure round it. We design the vision of the materials and finishes in the design studio, considering the layering and textures of fabrics, materials and wallcoverings as our starting point. Wallcovering can often be left to the end of the design process, but in fact it should be considered from the beginning with the hard and soft materials, as it is the skin of the room or space. This stunning space is overexposed with natural light and quantity of glass so we specified the Eri wallcovering to showcase as a unique object, a pure and texturised weave silk.

**What are your tips for layering multiple textures in a neutral-toned space?**
When designing in tones, the layering and textures are even more sensitive, yet critical to the success of the space. A fine balance between flatweaves, textures and overwoven materials is a lovely way to build the story. When using tones, grounding the body of the space with a mixture of soft and hard materials is important to give the space foundation and depth.

**What are your tips for decorating a ceiling?**
The ceiling, just like the floor and walls, should be considered as an equal partner in the 3D awareness and a key element of the interior. The interior architectural ceiling detail was installed to give the social area within the lounge balance and symmetry in a space that was off-centre. The use of abstract champagne gold leaf in an overlaid approach ensures the integrity of the contemporary styling of the interior yet adds a glamorous touch! When considering contrast finishes on the ceiling elevation, consider small pattern repeats, fine geometrics and tonal textures. it is important to reflect calm and balance to the ceiling to ensure your subconscious feels welcome in the interior space.

# THE ART OF

—

CHAPTER 3

—

# THE PATTERN CLASH

When two prints are better than one

# DECADENT LAYERED PATTERNS

—

The Hotel Maison Nabis in Paris is a prime example of how to layer patterns to create a decadent but intimate setting. Each room of the hotel follows a totally unique palette, allowing for endless colour and pattern combinations while still aligning in terms of style. The overarching theme of the hotel's design was inspired by the rich tones of precious gemstones.

Though the design may seem complex, the firm that executed the project, Maison Numéro 20, employed a simple formula to create a sense of cohesion between the separate spaces. They cleverly used the same wallcovering in different colourways to create iterations of a singular design. For example, a leafy palm frond print and a chinoiserie-inspired floral print are reimagined in an amethyst tone, ruby red and emerald shades to reflect the palette of each bedroom. In contrast, they employed a wavy champagne-toned graphic print behind each bed as a neutral foil, allowing the bright colours to meld without seeming overwhelming.

—
**DESIGNER**
Oscar Lucien Ono for
Maison Numéro 20

—
**LOCATION**
France

To visually connect the bedrooms to the public spaces, which are equally as extravagantly conceived, they repeated some of the same patterns, but in richer colours. We see the same wavy graphic print in a deep-turquoise tone, adding a sense of repetition and consistency within the extravagantly decorated space.

# ROOM OF CONTRASTS

—

The International Interior Design Exhibition was a showcase of interior design held in Brussels, Belgium, featuring the most celebrated designers and decorators across Europe and round the globe. Owing to the format of the exhibition, the designer, Benedetti Interieur, had only a single room to communicate the ethos of their brand, which specialises in window dressing, carpets and upholstered furniture. They chose to frame their mise-en-scène – a turquoise-coloured sectional sofa decked out with playful woven throw pillows, sculptural coffee tables and figurative art – with contrasting bold prints on the walls and ceiling. Above, they opted for an interlocking geometric pattern in a shade of green-blue and taupe, chosen to reflect the colour palette of the sofa and textiles set up below. Meanwhile, they dressed two symmetric wall panels with an illustrated pattern of large exotic florals in similar shades of green. These two seemingly opposing motifs worked in tandem to draw the eye in on the busy exhibition floor full to the brim with competing booths. Mixing these wallcovering patterns was a clever tactic to set themselves apart and showcase their unique style.

—
**DESIGNER**
Benedetti Interieur

—
**LOCATION**
Belgium

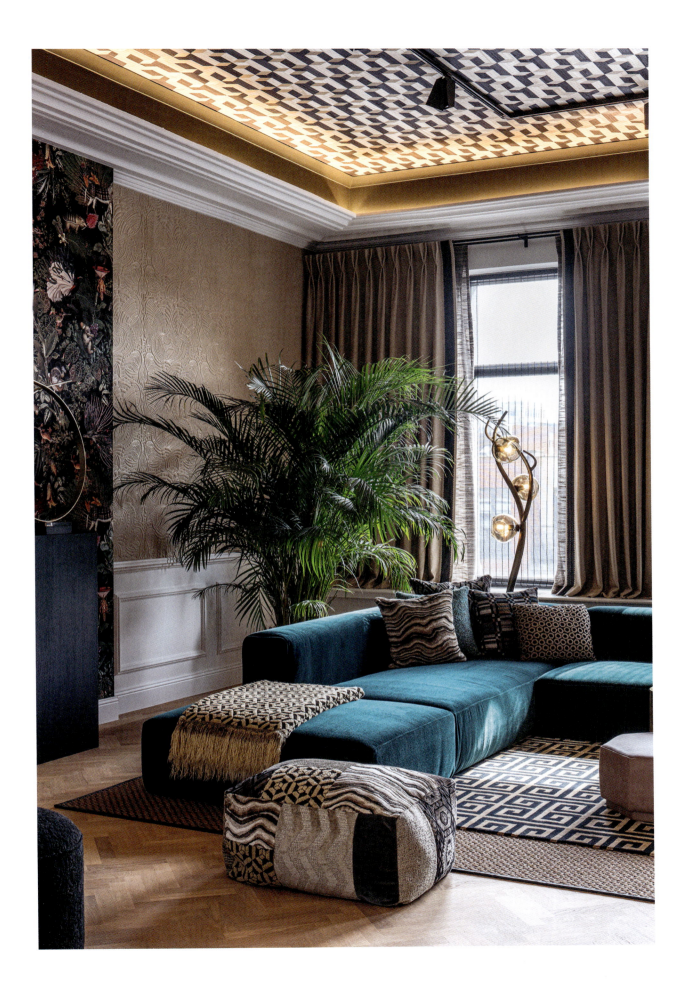

# DIFFERENTIATE SPACES BY WALLPAPER

—

Interior designer Jean Porsche is known for his riotous rooms that make use of every centimetre of space, layering boisterous patterns one on top of the other from floor to ceiling. This show flat in Málaga, Spain, is a slightly more restrained take on Porsche's signature style, but we can still see the customary clashing come into play.

On the walls, he used a subtle beige print reminiscent of a woven textile, which acts as a neutral canvas for the rest of the design flourishes within the space, such as moulded ceilings, statement furniture and bold, chevron-patterned rugs. In the kitchen, he introduced a more in-your-face wallcovering, which resembles rolling, plant-carpeted hills in shades of terracotta and grey. This accent wall not only works to add a pop of colour and pattern to the space, but also differentiates the kitchen from the seating area in the open-plan apartment – another practical application of clashing patterns in design.

—
**DESIGNER**
Jean Porsche
Arquitectura + Interiores

—
**LOCATION**
Spain

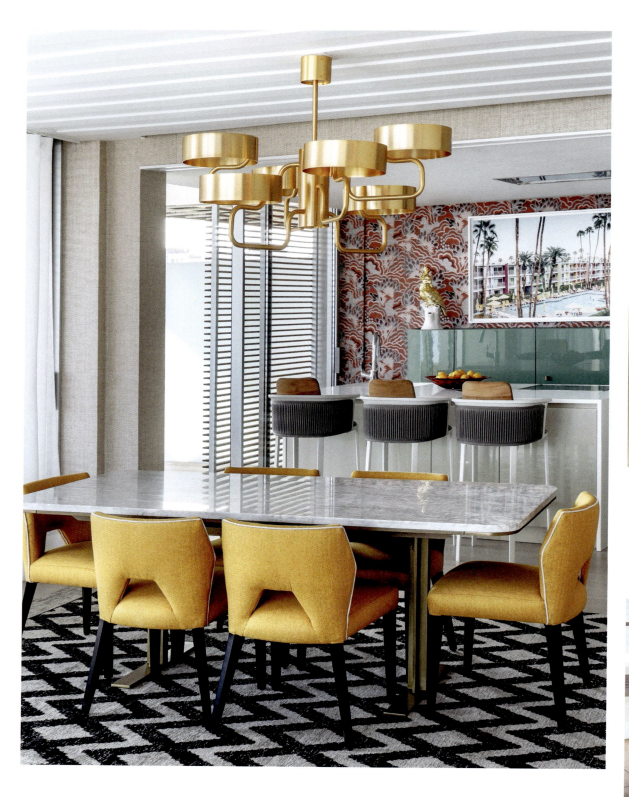

Layering patterns can be a tricky process, but here in the Edge Show Flat, designer Jean Porsche shows how it can be done with ease. Strong patterns on the carpets, throw pillows and kitchen accent wall contrast more subtle motifs on the moulded ceiling and grey textured walls.

# MULTIPLE MOTIFS MIXED

—

Designing a polished, elegant space doesn't mean you need to take the minimal route – an interior concept can feel simultaneously richly layered and refined. Such is the case with Lasan, a family-run Indian restaurant in Birmingham, England. Interiors studio Faber Design went completely maximal, creating a dining room that is undoubtedly a feast for the eyes. 'The design for Lasan emerged from a story about a family from India,' they explained regarding the concept. 'Capturing the true essence of India through their cuisine, our design weaves a narrative through the space.'

The designers mixed multiple motifs within the space, treating each element as a separate and surprising pop of pattern. For instance, in the main dining room, there are three panels, each featuring a different print – a blue-and-grey basketweave pattern, a hexagonal chequerboard-like print and a tangle of green ferns – that are used to frame family photos and other ephemera. The layering of all of these different elements works to create a sense of overall cohesion within the space while visually separating the various design elements. 'The wallcovering adds colour, texture and depth,' the designers add. 'It beautifully complements the decor, elevating traditional wall panels and creating the perfect backdrop to the artwork on display.'

—
**DESIGNER**
Faber Design

—
**LOCATION**
United Kingdom

The designers of Lasan Restaurant were able to elegantly tie together multiple patterns within the same room by using different prints that followed the shared colour palette of blue, turquoise and grey.

# BOLD, PLAYFUL, AND RISQUÉ

—

There is no better way to inject a sense of liveliness and personality into a hospitality project than filling it with eye-catching patterns. In the design of Vancouver's city centre retreat Hotel Belmont, designers Joanna Kado and Daniel Meloché took this idea and ran with it, creating a bold, playful space that's more than just a little risqué.

Not only are the walls rich with pattern and texture, but Meloché and Kado also took the clash concept one step further by decking out the floors and ceilings, too. They incorporated features such as terrazzo floors, chequerboard print tiles and colourfully veined marble in the dining room.

—

**DESIGNER**
Daniel Meloché Design
& Kado Design

—

**LOCATION**
Canada

While the pattern clashing in the reception and bar area is subtle, the designers deployed the technique to great effect. By mixing two bold patterns in different colours, another layer of depth and contrast is added to the already maximal space.

# DANIEL MELOCHÉ AND JOANNA KADO

Joanna Kado and Daniel Meloché met eleven years ago in a contest for British Columbia's best young designer, where they were challenged to design display suites on a tight budget for a local developer. They both beat the competition and landed the two top spots in the competition, giving them a lasting bond to this day. Over the years, they worked together in-house at a well-known hospitality design firm, where they both led multiple restaurant and hotel projects across North America. With twenty years of combined design experience and complementary styles, it was natural for Kado and Meloché to collaborate on projects, within the firm they worked for as well as outside it, in their own boutique design studios.

—
**BOLD,
PLAYFUL,
AND RISQUÉ**
Canada
—

**The project, in the designer's words:**
Our client envisioned a retro house party vibe that paid homage to the nostalgia of the 60s and the 70s, married with the camaraderie you experience at a house party. With a space on three levels containing multiple rooms, we designed 'The Basement', 'The Living Room', 'The Den' and 'The Kitchen' to be visually stimulating and photogenic from all angles. Our client wanted to ensure each vignette was Instagrammable and memorable to their guests.

**Take us through the design process of choosing the wallcovering for this project.**
Choosing wallcovering is always such an enjoyable process with the many options on the market. For this project, we specifically dived in searching for prints and colours that felt vintage and playful yet modern. We also wanted the wallcoverings to have a tactile texture to them to give dimension to the walls. One of the first patterns we selected was Avalon Flamingo, which helped pull our colour palette together.

**In the bar area you employed multiple different textures – from the wallcovering to the ceiling – but all in a similar shade of inky blue. What are some tips for mixing and matching different textures in the same colour palette?**
Layering textures is important to successful design, as it creates dimension in a room. We employed a bold colour palette of pinks, oranges, blues and black that complement each other in their intensity. We used some tone-on-tone patterns that give the illusion of texture while still adding patterns to the space. These tonal patterns allowed us to curate various textures together all in one space.

**Working within a space that has such bold features, such as the chequerboard flooring and marble fireplace, how do you introduce wallcovering that can hold its own?**
Finding the right balance and scale is key in a bold space. Giving enough breathing room between features really allows each focal point to stand on its own while working in harmony. For example, in 'The Den', we installed a bold terrazzo fireplace with the Avalon Flamingo wallpaper across from it. We separated the two with an ornately painted moulding to give that visual separation between patterns.

**What are your tips for choosing art, lighting and other decorative accessories to match a patterned wall?**
The accent decor in the space, such as lighting and art, should always complement the patterned wall finish. When using a simple and textured pattern, you can layer in more bold and eye-catching lighting or art. On the flip side, when using a bold pattern such as Avalon Flamingo, we recommend adding more subdued accents - such as an architectural mirror - so the pattern is not overshadowed in the space.

# MAXIMAL

—

CHAPTER 4

—

# THINKING

More is more in these eye-catching interiors

# WONDROUS LIVING ROOM

—

During the yearly Maison & Objet design fair in Paris, Eichholtz Interiors wanted to create a setting that would bring out the best of their sophisticated line of luxury furniture, lighting and home textiles. Since the furnishings that were on show conformed to a monochromatic white palette, the designers had some freedom in creating a more elaborate look for the walls. They chose a gorgeous forest scene at dusk to imbue a sense of calm and wonder within the space. Each part of the textile-based covering looks as if it were sewn in place by hand. The result channels the glamour of a Park Avenue penthouse or a Kensington townhouse, the ideal setting for the upscale furniture on display.

—
**DESIGNER**
Eichholtz Interiors

—
**LOCATION**
The Netherlands

The vertical lines made by the trees depicted in these gorgeous mural-like wallcoverings add a sense of verticality to the room, making the ceilings feel taller than they really are.

# MODERN ART DECO BAR

——

Creating a show-stopping cosmopolitan nightlife destination was the goal for this stunning bar in Zurich, Switzerland. 'The vision of the owners was to design an atmosphere that channels bar culture from big capitals such as New York and London,' the designers reveal regarding the brief they were given for the project. 'The design needed to be timeless and stylish with a modern art deco touch.' Composed of several intimate sections, the designers used multiple wallcoverings, all within a similar colour palette, to differentiate the spaces. For instance, in the central bar area, which the designers describe as the 'main stage', they covered the ceiling with a subtle patchwork floral pattern that resembles jacquard woven silk for a 'modern art deco style', which they bring down onto the wall in the seating area to visually connect the two spaces. Further along in the seating area, they added a light-blue palm print within a recessed arch to create an accent wall. Meanwhile, in the bathrooms, they went for a more playful, intimate feel by adding all-over jungle prints. As an added touch, they used the prints found in the bathroom for the bartenders' aprons, creating an all-round unforgettable experience.

——
**DESIGNER**
LIGNO in-Raum AG

——
**LOCATION**
Switzerland

A troupe of amber-coloured monkeys peek through bushes and trees in the bar bathroom. This choice of lively print, coupled with the room's low lighting, creates a striking and evocative atmosphere.

# INDUSTRIAL MEETS SPEAKEASY

—

The Lexy Club in Zurich, Switzerland, is an intimate basement bar with a lot of attitude. The club is billed as a late-night-to-early-morning dance bar where you can let your inhibitions run wild. 'At Lexy, electronic music sets the tone, while night-blue light made of geometric shapes illuminates your vision until the sun rises again,' the owners say of the concept. The night-blue geometric shapes they refer to are, in fact, a stylish vinyl wallcovering specially designed to look like patchwork fabric, which completes the industrial-meets-speakeasy vibe of the design. 'The selected wallpaper has perfectly fitted into the sophisticated light and shape concept for the club, giving the whole a very high-quality look,' they go on to say. The designers even included other elements within the space that complement the design, including similarly faceted mirrors and modular seating, creating an all-over patterned effect within the energy-packed space.

—
**DESIGNER**
Dyer-Smith AG

—
**LOCATION**
Switzerland

In a high-traffic space such as a nightclub, where spilled drinks and stray arms can spell trouble for walls and those charged with keeping them clean, wallcovering can provide a clever solution. A thick covering in a dark heavy-duty vinyl hides most accidents and keeps walls protected from damage.

# BASEMENT BAR

—

What may seem like a hidden speakeasy is in fact the basement of a private home. Designer Linda Lagrand was tasked with turning the space into a sophisticated lounge and bar with an adjacent wine room. 'We really wanted to bring the club feeling into this space,' says Lagrand. 'The residents host parties and wine and champagne tastings here, so the atmosphere had to match with that function. Luxury, international, night club, glamour: those are the keywords we started from.'

'The empty walls of the basement came to life by applying textured wallcovering,' Lagrand describes of the design. 'By using dark colours, you create an intimate atmosphere. The wallcovering was applied as panelling to transform the square, empty space into a classic gentlemen's club. The metamorphosis of this space was truly enormous, and the wallcovering played a big role in this transformation. In the wine room, we used cork wallpaper behind the wine closet – the link with wine and champagne bottles is obvious!'

—

**DESIGNER**
Linda Lagrand

—

**LOCATION**
The Netherlands

The textured brown-toned wallcovering that Lagrand chose for the basement bar makes the low-lit space feel like a sophisticated secret speakeasy.

# NATURAL CLASS

—

Designer Christine Jahan pulled out all the stops when renovating this charming Federal-style house in Pasadena, California. She filled the home with light, colour and art, creating a richly layered space that she describes as 'natural class'. For the wallcovering that was used across the open-plan ground floor, Jahan opted for a 'multidimensional grey wallpaper with subtle hints of pink,' she says. 'The texture livened up the walls, contrasting beautifully with the high-gloss white trim.'

Jahan explains that she used this wallcovering because it felt alive and fitted perfectly into her concept: 'It isn't just a textured wallpaper that mimics silk. It is visually multidimensional and it provokes an emotion from those who experience it in person. Even before the floors were done and the windows were untaped from painting, the entire room felt alive when covered with the wallcovering on every wall. People would gasp when they entered the space, and I'm not even sure they knew why they liked it so much. Bringing in furnishings and accessories that pulled out the hidden and subtle colours of the wallcovering served to raise the depth and energy of the original concept even more.'

—
**DESIGNER**
Christine Jahan
Designs

—
**LOCATION**
United States

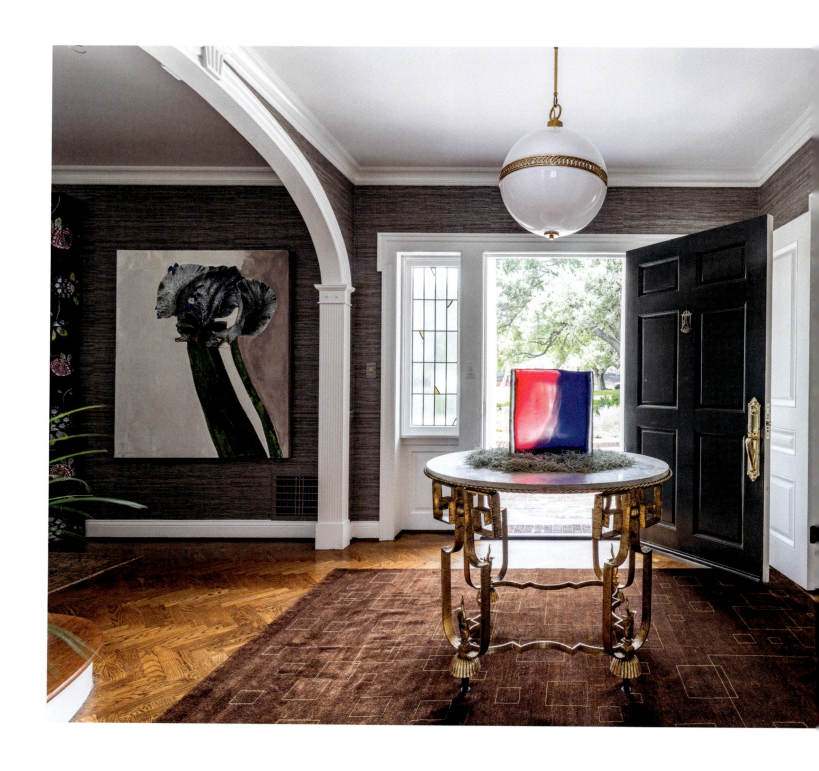

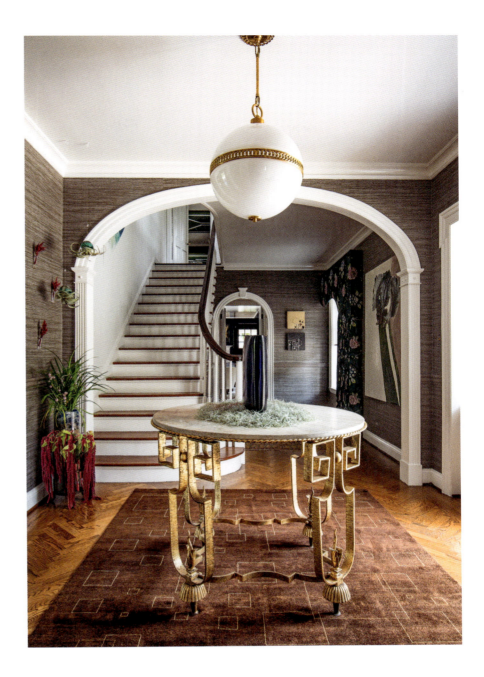

The grey-toned wallcovering's subtle gradient provided the perfect canvas for the homeowners' eclectic collection of art and design. A mix of bright abstract paintings, antique rugs and ornate vintage brass mirrors, plus lots and lots of bright flowers, bring this noble historic house into the present day.

# A WORLD JOURNEY WITHIN A RESTAURANT

—

Set in the historical centre of 's-Hertogenbosch in The Netherlands, The Shoege, an inventive restaurant with an international flair, is housed in a listed building originally constructed in 1719. In developing the concept for the space, the designers, Smaek Design, wanted to pay tribute to the historic original location, while creating an exciting interior that also felt completely modern, playful and new. In that sense, the starting point for the design was a 'culinary world journey,' explain the designers. 'We translated this concept to the interior design, the recipes and the different styles. A multitude of ingredients, materials, patterns and colours, used even in the smallest details, underline this worldly kitchen.'

The wallpaper in the dining room was applied as a 'trigger piece', a piece of art 'in the front of this restaurant, beautifully lighted and clearly visible for passers-by,' the designers explain. 'We chose a wallpaper with a story that was full of colours, botanicals, nature and diversity.' The pattern features flowers and animals on a gold-toned background, an eye-catching contrast to the historic building's sturdy wooden architecture. 'You can look at it for hours, talk about it, and you discover something else each time. It's comparable to the diversity in humanity and the storytelling of this culinary world journey,' they add.

—
**DESIGNER**
Smaek Design
Marieke Prudon

—
**LOCATION**
The Netherlands

Pink and gold are the perfect mix for this lively restaurant in The Netherlands. The winding vines that decorate the rattan lampshades in the dining room cleverly reference the wallcovering's tropical theme, making guests feel as if they've stepped into a fantastical jungle.

# CHRISTIE WRIGHT

—

Since 2021, Christie Wright has been the art director for Dutch lifestyle brand Moooi. Besides curating the design pieces in the Moooi collection, she is also the creative mind behind the brand's design language. The successful Museum of Extinct Animals design language was developed under her artistic direction, firmly establishing Moooi as a lifestyle brand. Extinct Animals inspired multiple multisensorial collections for surfaces such as fabrics, wallcoverings, carpets and accessories. She is also the driving force behind the brand's extraordinary collaborations with artists and designers from all over the world, further expanding the multisensorial world of Moooi.

—
## MOOOI
The Netherlands
—

# MOOOI, IN THE DESIGNERS' WORDS:

**How would you describe your, and Moooi's, design style?**
Original, unexpected, inspiring, eclectic and provocative. We are serious about design but playful in our approach. We work with designers globally and try to make their design dreams come true. To create the unexpected welcome and elicit the extra 'Ooh!' in terms of beauty and uniqueness. To create a multisensory and comprehensive lifestyle collection that inspires a life extraordinary!

**Take us through your process of designing a wallcovering. Where do you start?**
In 2018, we introduced our new artistic direction for the brand with our presentation of The Museum of Extinct Animals. We found inspiration in forgotten species that continue to live in our memories and imagination. From there, we created a surface collection of wallcoverings, carpets, leathers and fabrics that brought these animals back to life. With each design, we take our animal muse and study its behaviours, its history and its personality, and translate it into a design. From the dance of the Calligraphy Bird that creates calligraphy-like strokes on surfaces with its tail to attract a mate, to the layers of green on the Blushing Sloth that accumulate on the fur to create a layered richness of textures and colours.

**Where do you find inspiration for both the pattern and the colour palette?**
Sometimes inspiration comes in the most unexpected ways. A few years ago, we encountered this new revolutionary denim out of Japan that was developed for applications outside of its typical use. This material not only inspired direct use in upholstery applications on furniture; we also jumped to the wall, inspiring an entire wallcovering collection we named Tokyo Blue. We drew our inspiration from its Japanese origin in terms of pattern development. Colours were derived from its denim roots – indigos, acid-washed blues, midnight denims, pops of red and copper embroidery detail. We also used complementary materials such as tatami weavings and wooden veneer finishes to complete the collection. We elevated denim, a common material, to become a beautiful luxurious material for interiors.

**What are your tips for choosing the right kind of wallcovering for a space?**
Many people see wallcovering as the final touch to an interior. We like to turn the process upside down and let the wallcovering be the first selection in our interior and build the mood round this. Patterns are rich in the stories they tell. They attract the eye and let the mind wander. We bring our own individual interoperation to the designs and build our own interior narratives from these starting points.

# MODERN

—

## CHAPTER 5

—

# ELEGANCE

Classic designs reimagined for the present day

# GLAMOROUS AUTUMN

—

Oasis Srl is a well-known luxury design brand. In creating the concept for their latest showroom, their goal was to highlight the sumptuous materials used to fashion their furniture and lighting products. They chose an earthy, autumnal palette of browns, oranges and blacks to highlight the collection. 'The dark-brown fine-wood finishes combined with the rusty-orange velvet of the chairs and exquisite bronze details create a welcoming and refined space, instilling a feeling of ecstatic relaxation,' the design team describes of their concept.

In choosing the wallcovering, they went for natural motifs that would complement but not overpower the objects. For example, in the main section of the showroom, a muted pattern of fanning ferns was used in a mise-en-scène meant to highlight a pair of black leather armchairs, a console and an art deco inspired mirror. The understated pattern provides the perfect background to understand how Oasis's products can be styled at home. 'Thanks to its high quality and its elegant design pattern, it perfectly matches Oasis products, conferring a prestigious and coordinated total look throughout the room. The Oasis installation seeks to combine the glamorous metropolitan vibe with the enchantment of nature, creating a cosy yet prestigious environment capable of surprising every day,' says the team.

—
**DESIGNER**
Oasis Srl

—
**LOCATION**
Italy

The soft, sweeping curves of the fern-patterned wall-covering provide a subtle juxtaposition to the strict, straight-lined geometries of the furniture. However, the lacquered wooden framing that encloses the wallcovering adds a sense of structure, tying the entire interior concept together.

# LUXE AND LOW-KEY HOTEL

—

There's no better way to tie together a richly layered room than by adding a lushly patterned wallcovering. This sitting room in Paris's Hôtel Henriette finds the perfect balance between luxe and low-key, and the designers' choice of wallcovering proves it. Within the reception area, they chose two contrasting motifs. The first is a grey-toned foliage pattern, which acts as a subtle canvas for the navy-blue walls and sophisticated floating pendant lamps. The second, and the bolder of the two, is an asymmetric patchwork pattern in a shimmering shade of sapphire, which makes the gold-toned furnishings pop against the deep blue. Within the hotel rooms, they swapped this colour scheme to striking effect. Behind the bed, the wall is covered with the same patchwork pattern as the reception area, except this time in a glittering shade of gold with navy-blue accents on the wall. The sophisticated use of contrasting colours, patterns and tones has resulted in a gorgeous design concept that feels like an updated take on classic Parisian style.

—
**DESIGNER**
Hôtel Henriette

—
**LOCATION**
France

The sumptuous mix of patterns, noble materials such as marble, vintage furniture and elegant bronze accents imbues the rooms of this Parisian hotel with a sense of art deco glamour.

# Functional luxury

—

Designers Studio de Blieck were tasked with transforming this long-time family home into a warm and sophisticated retreat for the owners, whose children have moved out and started families of their own. They wanted to add a sense of luxury to the space while still retaining its functionality for when their grandchildren come to visit.

One of the things the clients wanted was to make a space for the husband where he could entertain and unwind. 'The idea of the space was to create a "gentleman's room" – chic, with international grandeur,' explain the architects. 'The design and the material for this extraordinary wallcovering have been the basis of the entire ground floor.' The playful forest pattern was the perfect choice for the husband's room while remaining in the same colour palette as the rest of the house so the room does not feel visually separated. For example, in the bedroom, the designers used two different but complementary grey-toned textile wallcoverings. Behind the bed, an abstract python-patterned wallcovering in lush velvet contrasts with the woodgrain motif behind the television and fireplace, creating a subtle layered effect that perfectly matches the colour scheme of the rest of the house.

—
**DESIGNER**
Studio de Blieck

—
**LOCATION**
The Netherlands

Within the bedroom and living room, the designers opted for wallcoverings that would complement the many layers of textiles within these two spaces. The patterns, textures and motifs are all defined by the same pale-grey colour palette, which allows the disparate elements to live in harmony with one another.

# HISTORIC HOTEL WITH CONTEMPORARY FEATURES

—

This chic hotel in the heart of Bordeaux was designed with luxury in mind. It is set in a historic building with decadent original features, so the designers created a vibrant mix of contemporary and classic elements. For example, each of the common areas follows a different colour palette. In the reception area, the jumping-off point was a boldly patterned wallcovering featuring a graphic gold art deco inspired pattern, which they both used behind the desk and also chose to transform into a runner to cover the marble floors. They then added gold-toned accessories to further emphasise the effect. Meanwhile, in the dining room, the concept is all about blue. A decadent marble print wallcovering was installed in the moulded wall panels, acting as a veritable art piece itself.

—
**DESIGNER**
Oscar Lucien Ono
for Maison Numéro 20

—
**LOCATION**
France

Working with classic design elements doesn't mean a space has to feel stuffy. If using decorative features such as wall mouldings and wainscoting, try balancing these more traditional elements with a vibrant and eye-catching palette of bold colours and strong patterns.

# PLAYFUL HOME OFFICE

—

'I've had a home office for years, but I wasn't happy with it,' says blogger and interior designer Elisah Jacobs, who recently went about giving her at-home workspace a total makeover. 'It should be much more inspiring, especially because it's my office and I'm there every day. I decided to change the space drastically, with a warm-red colour on the walls, new furniture and a playful way to make the arch stand out more. It used to be the passage to the room behind it, but it was closed by the former inhabitants, so I accentuated the arch with a monkey-patterned wallcovering. This wallcovering is a perfect fit. It is extra artsy because of the denim and the embroidery. You just keep looking lovingly at this print of Asian landscapes and monkeys, discovering something new each time. Over the next few years, our interior will keep changing, but this artsy wall will always stay.' Alternatively, in her child's bedroom, she used a similarly fun print: a sophisticated foliage pattern in a matte gold tone that can easily grow with the child from baby's room to kid's space.

—

**DESIGNER**
Elisah Jacobs
Interior Junkie

—

**LOCATION**
The Netherlands

# CREATIVE WORKSPACE

—

There's no reason for the interior design of an office to be dull.
A playful, colourful space is much more conducive to creative work. Case in point, the office of interior designers Theo-Bert Pot and Jelle Van de Schoor, who transformed the ground floor of his own home into his new headquarters. Pot used every opportunity he could to add colour, patterns and life to the space, but the most stunning elements are certainly the walls. In the main reception area, he covered the entire wall, which frames an ornately carved fireplace, with a dreamy hilly scene that looks as if it were painted in situ. He then matched the pinkish tone of the wallcovering to the original wood-plank floors, which he painted a dusty shade of rose.

In the workspaces, he went for a comparably more subdued concept, but still teeming with life. The walls were painted a deep shade of forest green, save for a single accent wall above the second fireplace.
He opted for an ultra-contemporary yellow-and-gold motif, which adds a layer of interest without being overpowering. The perfect setting to let your creativity run free.

—
**DESIGNER**
Theo-Bert Pot &
Jelle Van de Schoor

—
**LOCATION**
The Netherlands

THE MAVERICK SOUL

JOHN RICHARDSON | AT HOME

THE TOUCH

THE NICE STUFF COLLECTOR 21

Pot and Van de Schoor carefully coordinated sightlines between spaces to always include a vibrant pop of colour or a vivacious print. From one of the ground-floor sitting rooms, where the walls are painted a muted shade of pink, a boisterous pattern featuring jungle plants is visible through the doorway, adding a nice sense of contrast between the rooms.

# THE NOTARY'S HOUSE

—

Colour is the main character in this grand family home in Utrecht by Norwegian designer Linda Lagrand. What was once a notary's office and mayor's home was transformed into a sumptuous residence by the Rotterdam-based designer. Throughout the house, the rooms are full of colour and life, but it is in the private spaces that true luxury reigns.

In designing the primary bedroom, Lagrand says they chose the colour palette first. 'We wanted to make it feel like a rich hotel suite,' she explains of the choice of colour, a deep aubergine. 'Since we like to work with natural materials and colours from nature, we thought the burgundy would enhance the room.' For the wallcovering, Lagrand continued with the theme of natural materials. She chose a woven diamond pattern made out of sisal, a type of agave plant from southern Mexico whose strong fibres make for long-wearing and sturdy textiles. Panels of the woven sisal were then framed within the wall moulding to break up the height of the ceilings and centre the placement of the bed, creating a sense of symmetry in the room. From there, she chose textiles and furnishings to complement the colourful walls, deftly mixing texture and pattern to grand effect.

—
**DESIGNER**
Linda Lagrand

—
**LOCATION**
The Netherlands

# LINDA LAGRAND

—

Linda Lagrand started Lagrand Interiors in 2010 after someone at a dinner party asked what she would do if it could be anything. The next day she enlisted for design education, and her days haven't felt like work ever since. Lagrand Interiors stands for tranquillity, colour and the boutique hotel feeling at home. By using muted colours that stem from nature, we design warm spaces that make you feel at home instantly. For the past twelve years, Lagrand has created numerous residential and commercial interiors where the five-star hotel experience resonates. Her Norwegian roots bring her to nature, her Rotterdam location adds sparkle and dynamics, and her love for art and craftsmanship is the finishing touch to her signature look.

—
**THE NOTARY'S HOUSE**
The Netherlands
—

**The project, in the designer's words:**
This was quite a classical, older building. It had been used in the beginning as a private home, then later it was used for a notary's office and the mayor's house. We wanted to bring back the classical details they used to have at that time, but we didn't want to do it in a classical way. That meant putting wallpaper in the frames on the wall in a contemporary colour palette. We chose burgundy because it felt both natural and rich – like a luxury hotel suite.

**How do you go about modernising such a classical building?**
The fact about these old buildings, at least here in The Netherlands, is that they have these high ceilings. You have more to work with, but you also have to do more to make it feel like an intimate bedroom, because they are so high and the rooms are so big. The panels with wallcovering inside are a great way to break up the height of the ceiling and make the room feel more cosy.

**How do you mix patterns while still creating a calm space?**
We like to do tone-on-tone in our rooms, which means colours that are quite near to one another, but also using materials and patterns that are quite opposite and contradictory. For example, even though we use a lot of patterns – we have a pattern in the floor carpet; we have patterns on the upholstery on the bench next to the bed, in the curtains, in the chair next to the vanity table – because they all have similar tones, they work together very well. Then the wallcovering is the element that ties everything together; it brings a classical feeling to the room.

**How could someone replicate your design process at home?**
What we do is called a material and colour study, which we do for every room. We want the feeling to be the same in the whole house, so even if you walk from a blue room to this burgundy room, you still have the same feeling of calmness and peace. When we are in the studio, we will have all the samples and all the fabrics and we will put them together on a table to see if it's okay, this works; this doesn't work. It allows us to see how all of the fabrics and textures will work together before installing them. This way, we are sure we've chosen the right wallcovering for the project, because we know that the rest of the textiles will work well with it. It's like making a mood board but for materials.

**What are your tips for a first-time decorator choosing a wallcovering?**
My advice would be to embrace the idea of wallcovering. Don't just put it on the wall behind your bed in your bedroom or the sofa in your living room. Covering an entire room with wallpaper makes the space feel as if it is embracing you; there is a much greater feeling of unity. It creates much more of a luxurious feeling when the walls are tactile, compared with when they are just smooth and painted.

# GRAPHIC

—

CHAPTER 6

—

# TOUCHES

Accent walls that steal the show

# LUXURY FARMHOUSE

—

'With the renovation of this old farm we created a real family house,' says Studio La Plume, who is responsible for this luxury farmhouse conversion in The Netherlands. 'The large spaces of the former farming company required a professional restyling to make it a cosy whole. The building is now an atmospheric house where all family members have their own space.' In the primary bedroom, the designers made the unconventional choice of aligning the bed in the centre of the room, against a wall that divides the A-frame loft into a sleeping area and closet. In order to attract the eye and give some weight to the added surface, they decorated the wall with a metallic textile covered in a repetitive cube pattern, a striking contrast to the natural materials and understated finishing found throughout the rest of the room. They then highlighted the luxe addition with a series of floating pendant lamps that beautifully reflect the metallic threads.

—

**DESIGNER**
Studio La Plume

—

**LOCATION**
The Netherlands

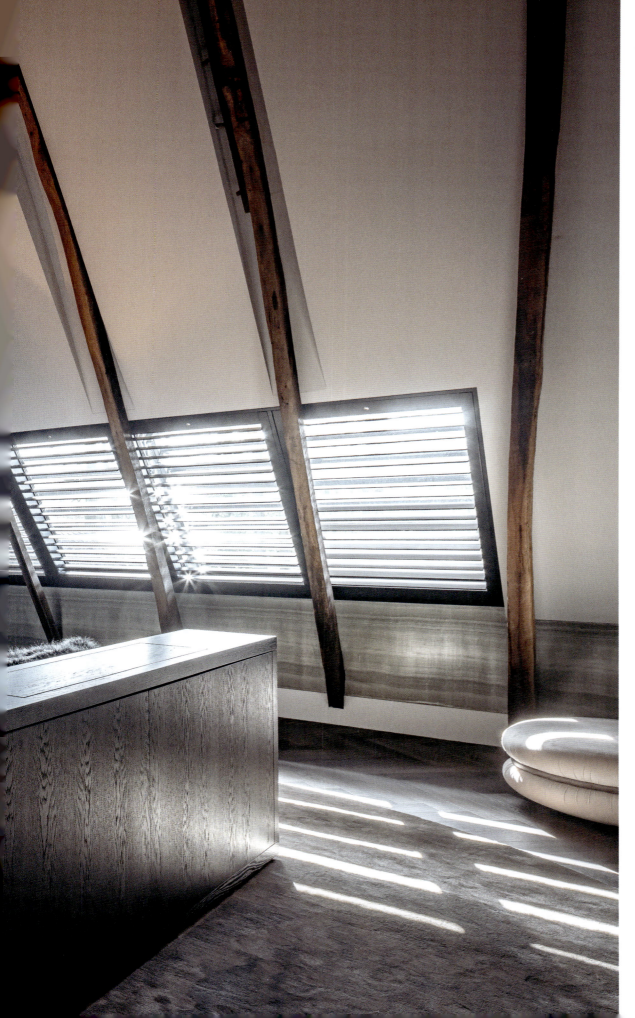

The metallic sheen of the woven textile wallcovering gorgeously reflects the soft amber-coloured light emitted from the sunburst-shaped pendant lamps.

# ART ON DISPLAY

—

When a home centres on an impressive collection of art, what better way to design the interior than to make the walls a piece of art themselves? This home by JAB Design Group in Princeton, New Jersey, is a great example of turning a canvas into a masterpiece. 'Foyers can be one of the most difficult spaces to design, often restricted by passageways and doorways,' explains the designer. 'So from the start of our concept we defined the design direction as walls first then all else to follow. We chose to make the three-storey wall a major feature by covering it with a strong chevron pattern to unify the levels.'

Elsewhere, they kept the walls neutral by using a textile wallcovering in both taupe and dark grey. The contrast, they say, 'defined the architecture and created intimate visuals supporting the seating, artwork and rugs.'

—
**DESIGNER**
JAB Design Group

—
**LOCATION**
United States

The bold black-and-white chevron-patterned wallcovering acts as a signpost for the eye, drawing visitors' gaze upwards to the top of the staircase. This optical effect gives the double-height space an even greater sense of verticality and brings attention to the framed photograph that hangs adjacent to the landing.

# THE CEILING SETS THE TONE

—

'Wallcoverings are one of our favourite accents in a space. They enhance a room in many ways, including adding unique texture, bold pattern or pops of fun colour,' say Daniel Meloché and Joanna Kado, who did exactly that at the Loft Lounge in Vancouver, British Columbia. For the design of this project, they decided to focus their energy upwards, decorating the ceiling in a blue-and-yellow graphic print wallcovering. Indeed, the ceiling sets the tone for the design of the entire space. The team even pulled colours from the pattern to use on the furniture – for example, the electric-blue booths and yellow textile accents throughout the space. 'Wallcovering takes what can be a plain wall or ceiling and adds life to the room overall," they add.

—
**DESIGNER**
Daniel Meloché Design
& Kado Design

—
**LOCATION**
Canada

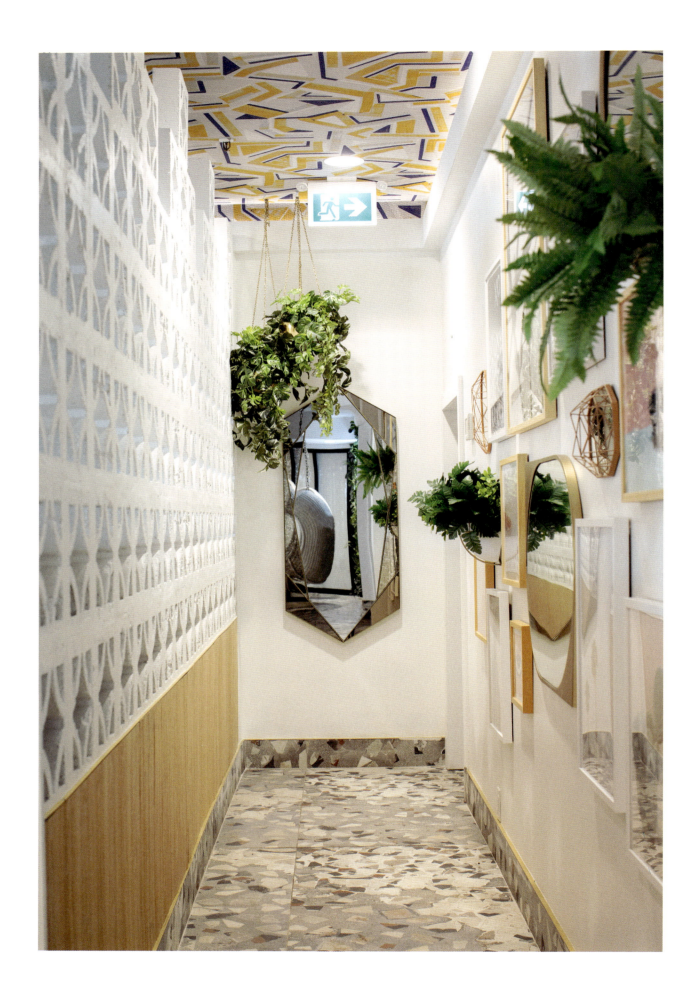

The designers made the decision to leave the restaurant's walls a simple, unfussy white, which gives the patterned ceiling a bit of room to breathe and allows the space to feel light and airy. In the bathroom, however, they chose a palm frondprinted wallcovering, which contrasts nicely with the pale-pink tilework on the wall.

# Colour-Blocked Hotel Room

—

To make the walls in this hotel room in Munich stand out, the designers chose to paint a playful, colour-blocked motif behind the bed, effectively making an abstracted art wall. 'The choice of colours is strong and is reflected in geometric shapes,' say the designers. 'The shapes form a kind of cocoon in the area round the beds, which creates a feeling of security.' As a source of contrast, they added a 3D textile wallcovering on the headboard, which adds an extra layer of texture. 'The headboard should be implemented with a simple solution and at the same time have a powerful effect. The fabric-like material also creates a sense of comfort.'

—
**DESIGNER**
Mery Reif –
Lova Design

—
**LOCATION**
Germany

There is no hard-and-fast rule that says wallcoverings must be used only on walls. The designers were creative in designing this hotel room bed, whose headboard is swathed in a 3D chevron-patterned wallcovering.

# ECLECTIC ACCENT WALL

—

'The design concept for this show apartment in London was young, eclectic, a bold, bright and colourful scheme,' explains the team behind Happy Place Design, who outfitted this apartment with a young design-savvy resident in mind. 'We selected this wallpaper because of its striking large-scale geometric design. We wanted the bedroom to be a strong statement with a young and edgy feel. The coral and lustrous metallic pink are fresh and bold, contrasting beautifully with the luxurious electric-blue velvet headboard we designed.' The concept is certainly not for the faint of heart, but for the right person, an outgoing accent wall is the way to go. 'Fortunately, our client likes bold colours, so we endeavoured to provide this in an elegant and sophisticated way,' they add.

—

**DESIGNER**
Happy Place Design

—

**LOCATION**
United Kingdom

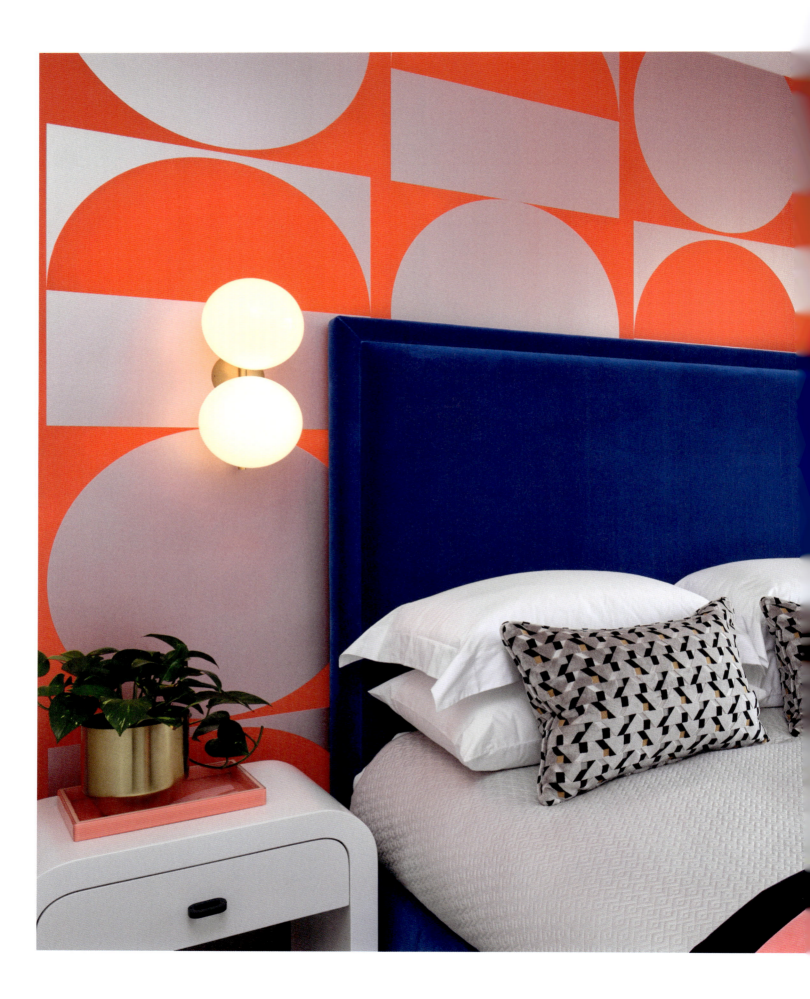

Despite the small size of the room, the large scale of the pattern tricks the eye into feeling as if the room is bigger than it really is. This colour-blocked eye-catcher was designed by Lenny Kravitz.

# A SPEAKEASY BAR

—

Domaine de la Timonerie is a luxury guest house in Baie de Somme, on the picturesque north coast of France. Here, in the bar area, the designers wanted to create a space where guests could unwind after a day spent exploring nearby nature reserves and the famous white-cliffed coastline. For the overall palette, they chose an understated slate grey offset by the occasional pop of gold to create a moody speakeasy vibe. To highlight the bar area they added a geometric, art deco inspired gold-patterned wallcovering as the visual focal point of the room, allowing this central feature to stand out against the low-key decor.

—

**DESIGNER**
Domaine de
la Timonerie

—

**LOCATION**
France

While both the bar and the fireplace feature a matching gold pattern that undeniably catches the eye, the designers chose a comparatively subtle wallcovering in a block print that resembles tiles for the remaining walls.

# GOLDEN EYE-CATCHER

—

'We often start from the wallcovering and choose all the home's colours round it,' reveals Paris-based designer Elodie Cottin regarding a tactic she and her team used to great effect in this Parisian family home. 'So the wallcovering choice is really important; it is an interesting starting point.' They found their inspiration in the metallic shades of this bold wallcovering, which they carried through to the rest of the house, adding gold touches throughout that refer back to the accent wall. 'It was very interesting, because the wallcovering has a really strong graphic pattern,' explains Cottin, 'with very present colour contrasts, black vs golden. This makes it a magnificent wallcovering. We wanted a wall with character, that immediately attracts the eye.'

—
**DESIGNER**
Studio Elodie Cottin

—
**LOCATION**
France

# EDGY DENIM WALLCOVERING

—

This interior design showcase in Spain takes the concept of the accent wall to the next level. The designers envisaged an entirely white room – including the walls, moulded ceiling, plush carpet and furniture – except for a single wall next to the bar, which they decorated with a 3D floral-patterned indigo wallcovering. More than just a colour scheme, the wallcovering is in fact made from denim fabric, which gives the wall an extra touch of edginess. The choice really makes the room pop and provides the perfect dose of colour and contrasting texture in an otherwise minimal design concept.

—
**DESIGNER**
Ele Room 62

—
**LOCATION**
Spain

The bright pop of indigo transforms an all-white zen-like space into a stylish sitting room that feels decidedly more contemporary and creative.

# NATURAL
# TOUCHES

—

'We did the entire restyling of this farmhouse,' explains the design firm
Studio La Plume, discussing this rugged yet cosy farmhouse in Drenthe.
'The most important part was to create a modern yet classic atmosphere.
It had to combine well with the existing elements of the farm. This resulted
in an atmospheric house with eye-catchers here and there.' Throughout the
house, they opted for natural textures and neutral shades – for example,
the reclaimed wooden beams that soar across the central areas.
The focal point of the living room, though, is undeniably the grand fireplace,
where the designers saw the opportunity to add some shine. They lined
the central wall with a stunning wallcovering, which, though it features a
pleated pattern, resembles the aged texture of the wooden beams.
'The wallpapers give the spaces just that little extra. They are the
eye-catchers of this house, in our opinion.'

—
**DESIGNER**
Studio La Plume

—
**LOCATION**
The Netherlands

The gold tones of the pleated wallcovering that lines
the fireplace were carried throughout thwe grand
living room in the form of brass-coloured accessories
and furniture.

# ADRIANA NICOLAU

———

Adriana Nicolau is one of Spain's most sought-after interior designers. Known for her playful yet sophisticated approach, her interiors are characterised by bright colours, rich finishings and an eclectic mix of art and furniture. Alongside her team, she has developed decor and interior design projects for residential and commercial clients from initial concept to complete execution, across Spain and Italy and further afield. Her studio, which is based in Madrid, specialises in contract, residential and retail design.

**How would you describe your style?**
My style is adaptable depending on the project I am facing. I am eclectic and elegant, with a fun point. Playing with colour is my weakness.

**In general, how can adding wallcovering enhance the design of a space?**
It absolutely transforms it. I like to take before and after pictures in spaces where just by changing the wallcovering it looks like a totally different room.

**Take us through the design process of choosing the wallcovering for these particular projects.**
Everything is usually born from an image that we want to show. Or, on the contrary, we have fallen in love with the paper and we see it as perfect for the place. Then it is shown to the clients, who are usually impressed and like it. In the case of the most daring, you have to work on the client a little more!

**When designing a room, how do you decide whether to incorporate all-over wallcovering or just an accent wall?**
I decide according to the size and the light. If it is a large space with good natural light, we go for a complete wallcovering, but if it is small or needs artificial light, we usually work with skirting boards or lighting. By backlighting the covering we can create very welcoming spaces.

**How do you choose the right kind of wallcovering for an accent wall?**
Well, you never know if it's the right one until you see the final result! I try to find out about the utility of the space in case it needs to be a moisture-resistant coating; otherwise, I can apply textiles. Then it is according to the client's specific taste. If we take into account all these factors, it usually turns out to be the right one.

**What are your tips for choosing the right placement of an accent wall?**
I pay close attention to whether it is visible at first sight to create that wow effect. A headboard can be a very effective placement, and one works well above a sink. Sometimes we look for a less-obvious space and give it some charm. In that case, it is best to take advantage of those hidden walls and give them personality with a nice wallpaper.

**What are your tips on lighting an accent wall?**
Obviously backlight it, so that the textures and all the beauty of the paper stand out well.

**INTRODUCTION**
p. 4 – 11 Courtesy of Arte

**FLORA & FAUNA**
p. 14 Courtesy of Arte
p. 16 – 21 Design by Atelier Gulla Jonsdottir;
Photography by Art Gray
p. 18 Courtesy of Arte
p. 22 – 27 Design by Barts Boekje
(www.instagram.com/bartsboekje); Photography by
Emma Peijnenburg (www.instagram.com/emmapeijnenburg)
p. 28 Courtesy of Arte
p. 28 – 33 Design & photography by Günel Aghazada
p. 34 – 39 Interior Architecture by Candice Bruny
(@candicebruny); Photography by Erick Saillet (@ericksaillet)
p. 43 Courtesy of Arte
p. 40 – 45 Design & Photography by Balo / Toon de Gruyter
p. 46 – 49 Design by Linda Lagrand Interiors;
Photography by Peter Baas
p. 50 – 57 Design by Traci Connell Interiors;
p. 50, 51, 56 Photography by Michael Hunter
p. 53 Courtesy of Arte
p. 54 Photography by Stephen Karlisch
p. 57 Photography by Kris Ellis

**STAYING NEUTRAL**
p. 58 Courtesy of Arte
p. 60 – 65 Design & photography by Interior Vitamins
p. 66 – 71 Design & Photography by Derenko Interior Design
p. 66 Courtesy of Arte
p. 72 – 77 Design by Maaike van Diemen;
Photography by Denise Zwijnen
p. 78 – 85 Design by Studio de Blieck;
Photography by Muk van Lil
p. 83 Courtesy of Arte
p. 86 – 91 Design & Photography by M&M Designs
p. 92 – 99 Design by Kris Turnbull Studios
(www.kristurnbull.com)

**THE ART OF THE PATTERN CLASH**
p. 100 Courtesy of Arte
p. 102 – 107 Design by Oscar Lucien Ono for Maison Numéro
20; photography by Didier Delmas
p. 108 – 113 Design by Benedetti Interieur
p. 110 Courtesy of Arte
p. 114 Courtesy of Arte
p. 114 – 119 Design by Jean Porsche Arquitectura + interiores
p. 120 – 125 Design by Faber Design; Photography by Richard
Southall / Emphasis Photography
p. 126 – 133 Design by Daniel Meloché Design and Kado
Design; Photography by Heather Merenda
p. 132 Courtesy of Arte

**MAXIMAL THINKING**
p. 134 Courtesy of Arte
p. 136 – 139 Design by Eichholtz Interiors
p. 140 – 145 Design by LIGNO in-Raum AG;

Photography by Gian Marco Castelberg;
Operator Dirk Hany & team
p. 146 – 151 Design by Dyer-Smith AG;
Photography by Patrick Armbruster
p. 152 – 157 Design by Linda Lagrand Interiors;
Photography by Peter Baas
p. 158 – 163 Design by Christine Jahan Designs;
Photography by Cristopher Nolasco
p. 164 - 168 Interior Design, concept, styling & management
by Smaek Design Marieke Prudon; Photography by Hidde(n)
Visuals Ibiza Modern Elegance
p. 169 Photography by Moooi (@moooi)

**MODERN ELEGANCE**
p. 170 Courtesy of Arte
p. 172 – 177 Design by Oasis Srl (www.oasisgroup.it)
p. 178 – 183 Hôtel Henriette, (www.hotelhenriette.com)
p. 184 – 189 Design by Studio de Blieck; Published in the Art
of Living, nr 4 2019
p. 190 – 193 Design by Oscar Lucien Ono for Maison
Numéro 20; Photography by Didier Delmas
p. 194 Courtesy of Arte
p. 194 – 197 Design by Elisah Jacobs (www.interiorjunkie.com)
p. 198 – 203 Design by Theo-Bert Pot & Jelle Van de Schoor;
Styling and Photography by Theo-Bert Pot (The Nice Stuff
Collector)
p. 204 – 209 Design by Linda Lagrand Interiors;
Photography by Space Content Studio
p. 208 Courtesy of Arte

**GRAPHIC TOUCHES**
p. 210 Courtesy of Arte
p. 212 – 215 Design by Studio La Plume; Photography
by Peter Baas
p. 216 – 221 Design by JAB Design Group;
Photography by Mike van Tassell
p. 222 – 227 Design by Daniel Meloché Design and
Kado Design; Photography by Janis Nicolay
p. 228 – 231 Design by Mery Reif, Lova Design;
Photography by Thomas Oberniedermayr
p. 232 – 235 Design by Happy Place Design Ltd.;
Photography by Bruno Rondinelli
p. 236 – 239 Domaine de la Timonerie, Bed & Breakfast in
the Somme Bay (FR); Photography by Sophie Boussahba
p. 240 – 243 Design by Studio Elodie Cottin;
Photograhpy by Agathe Tissier
p. 244 – 247 Bang & Olufsen space by Ele Room 62 at Casa
Decor 2020; Photography by Nacho Uribesalazar for Casa
Decor
p. 247 Courtesy of Arte
p. 248 – 251 Design by Studio La Plume;
Photography by Peter Baas
p. 252 – 253 Design by Adriana Nicolau;
Photography by Paloma Pacheco

**Texts**
Laura May Todd

**Editing**
Amy Haagsma

**Book Design**
Tina Smedts – De Poedelfabriek


Sign up for our newsletter with news about new and forthcoming publications on art, interior design, food & travel, photography and fashion as well as exclusive offers and events. If you have any questions or comments about the material in this book, please do not hesitate to contact our editorial team: art@lannoo.com


©Lannoo Publishers, Belgium, 2022
D/2022/45/340 – NUR450/454
ISBN 978-94-014-8363-6
www.lannoo.com

wallcoverings for the ultimate in refinement